W9-AHR-869

POLICE CARS

Please visit our web site at: www.garethstevens.com
For a free color catalog describing Gareth Stevens Publishing's
list of high-quality books and multimedia programs,
call 1-800-542-2595 or fax your request to (414) 332-3567.

Library of Congress Cataloging-in-Publication Data available upon request from publisher.
Fax (414) 336-0157 for the attention of the Publishing Records Department.

ISBN 0-8368-3047-4

First published in 2002 by
Gareth Stevens Publishing
A World Almanac Education Group Company
330 West Olive Street, Suite 100
Milwaukee, WI 53212 USA

Text and photos: Eric Ethan
Cover design and page layout: Tammy Gruenewald

Printed in the United States of America

1 2 3 4 5 6 7 8 9 06 05 04 03 02

by Eric Ethan

Gareth Stevens Publishing
A WORLD ALMANAC EDUCATION GROUP COMPANY

These police cars are at a police station. Soon police officers will take them on patrol.

A police car has a siren and flashing lights. Can you find the siren on this car? Look closely at the front bumper.

All police cars have radios. Police officers use radios to talk to the police station and to each other.

This police officer is using her radio on patrol. The radio tells her where to go when there is an emergency.

This police car has a computer.
The computer gives the police officer
important information very quickly.

The engine in a police car is large,
so the car can go very fast.

A police officer always wears a seat belt. All police officers learn to drive safely.

A police car has first aid equipment in its trunk. Sometimes police officers must help people who are hurt.

This police officer is ready for duty!

GLOSSARY

bumper (BUM-per): a bar across the front or back of a car that protects the car if the car gets bumped.

emergency (ee-MER-gen-see): something that needs immediate attention.

equipment (ee-KWIP-ment): the tools a person uses to do a job.

patrol (pah-TROLL): driving around to make sure things are okay.

siren (SIE-ren): a machine that makes a loud warning noise.

MORE BOOKS TO READ

A Day with Police Officers. Hard Work (series). Jan Kottke (Children's Press)

Police Cars. Community Vehicles (series). Marcia S. Freeman (Pebble Books)

Police Cars. Transportation Library (series). Becky Olien (Bridgestone Books)

WEB SITES

Police Car Web Site
policecar.topcities.com/

Police Cars Photo Gallery
members.tripod.com/policecars/

INDEX